World of Music

Eastern Asia

Peter Gutiérrez

Heinemann
LIBRARY

www.heinemann.co.uk/library
Visit our website to find out more information about **Heinemann Library** books.

To order:
 Phone 44 (0)1865 888066
 Send a fax to 44 (0)1865 314091
 Visit the Heinemann Bookshop at www.heinemann.co.uk/library to browse our catalogue and order online.

First published in Great Britain by Heinemann Library,
Halley Court, Jordan Hill, Oxford, OX2 8EJ, part of
Harcourt Education.
Heinemann Library is a registered trademark of Harcourt
Education Ltd.

Editorial: Louise Galpine, Harriet Milles, and
         Rachel Howells
Design: Victoria Bevan and Philippa Baile
Illustrations: Jeff Edwards
Picture Research: Hannah Taylor and Fiona Orbell
Production: Julie Carter

Originated by Chroma Graphics (Overseas)
Pte Ltd
Printed and bound in Hong Kong

ISBN 978 0 4311 1779 9
12 11 10 09 08
10 9 8 7 6 5 4 3 2 1

British Library Cataloguing in Publication Data
Gutierrez, Peter
Eastern Asia. - (World of music)
780.9'5
A full catalogue record for this book is available from the
British Library.

Acknowledgements
The publishers would like to thank the following for
permission to reproduce photographs:
Alamy Images pp. **7 left** (China Span/Keren Su), **12**
(Chris Hammond), **29** (Christopher Pillitz); Corbis
pp. **5**, **43** (Reuters/Paul Yeung), **10** (epa/Rolex De
La Pena), **13** (John Van Hasselt), **14** (Free Agents
Limited), **17** (Michel Setboun), **19** (Reuters/Claro
Cortes IV), **20** (Hulton-Deutsch Collection), **27**
(epa/How Hwee Young), **28** (Michael Freeman), **31**
(epa/Geoff Caddick), **32** (Michael S. Yamashita), **33**
(Free Agents Limited), **37** (Reuters/Brian Snyder), **38**
(Barry Lewis); **42** Empics/AP; Getty Images pp. **7 right**
(AFP/Sanka Vidanagama), **8** (Junko Kimura), **24–25**
(DAGOC/Michael Steele), **35** (AFP/Laurent Fievet);
John Warburton-Lee Photography/David Fanshawe
p. **9**; Lebrecht/M. Nicolaou p. **34**; Lonely Planet/
Tom Cockrem p. **23**; OnAsia/Jerry Redfern p. **39**;
Panos/John Leo Dugast p. **6**; Photolibrary/JTB Photo
Communications Inc p. **22**; Redferns pp. **16** (Odile
Noel), **40** (Philip Ryalls), **41** (Mike Burnell); Reuters/
Gary Hershorn p. **36**; V&A Images p. **21**.

Cover photograph of woman playing a *koto* reproduced
with permission of Photolibrary (photodisc).

The publishers would like to thank Patrick Allen for his
assistance in the preparation of this book.

Every effort has been made to contact copyright holders
of any material reproduced in this book. Any omissions
will be rectified in subsequent printings if notice is given
to the publishers.

Contents

Some words will be printed in bold, **like this.** You can find out what they mean by looking in the glossary.

Music across the map

Welcome to East Asia! This large region is home to some of the world's oldest **cultures**. But it is also a place where technology pushes music into the future. As a result, modern teenagers treat some **pop music** stars as larger-than-life heroes.

East Asia stretches from Myanmar in the west to the edge of the Pacific Ocean. This large area contains a huge variety of music.

The cultures of East Asia have affected each other through centuries of trade, warfare, and travel.

Neighbours who share

Have you ever borrowed anything from a neighbour? People in East Asia have a long history of sharing sounds and instruments with each other.

China's neighbouring countries, such as Korea and Japan, often have similar music. Moving farther west, countries such as Thailand are more influenced by India. In the south of the region are Malaysia, Indonesia, and the Philippines. Their cultures reflect the contributions of travellers who stopped there over the years.

Music on the move

Music was so important to the kings of Laos that they went everywhere with musicians following them. This **orchestra**-on-the-go made up songs on the spot. It played bamboo flutes, gongs, and xylophones.

Today's pop music crosses borders. Rain is a star in Japan and China as well as in Korea.

Rain

The young South Korean performer Rain (born 1982) has won awards for his music videos as well as his television acting. When tickets to his concert in Tokyo, Japan, went on sale in 2005, fans bought all 11,000 tickets in less than 30 seconds!

Around Eastern Asia

With its large size and central location, China has had a strong effect on its neighbours in the region. At times it has actually controlled other lands. Today, for instance, China rules Tibet, which was a separate country until 1950.

For centuries Chinese people have believed that music is an important part of who they are. It helped join them together as a group. But Chinese **culture** also pays attention to foreign music and different instruments.

These three photos show different versions of a similar instrument. From left to right are the *khaen* from Laos and Northeast Thailand, the *sheng* from China, and the *sho* from Japan.

Taizong

Taizong was a Chinese emperor born in AD 599. He ruled from AD 626 until his death in AD 649. Taizong loved music so much that he had 10 different **orchestras**! They showed how the Chinese valued music from many parts of Asia and many different peoples. Eight of the orchestras featured musicians from other countries in East Asia or from different **ethnic groups** within China.

A *zither* is a plucked stringed instrument without a long neck. In China, a popular type is the *cheng*. Its cousins include the Japanese *koto*, the Korean *gayageum*, and the Vietnamese *dan tranh*. These similarities between instruments show how musicians from different lands have shared ideas over the centuries.

Playing by mouth

A harmonica contains many holes though which air can pass. It is part of the family of mouth organs. These types of instruments have separate pipes that produce different sounds. In Laos and Thailand, the *khaen* works somewhat like a harmonica. The Chinese based their own mouth organ on it.

Japan: a musical mixing pot

In East Asia, musical ideas often blend. A term such as "Japanese music" can mean something different to different people. Japanese **classical music** has some features of Chinese, Korean, and Indian music. In Okinawa, at Japan's southern tip, the region's **folk music** shows the influence of South-east Asia. **Western music** became widely popular in the 1800s. In this way, Japan has acted like a musical sponge, absorbing ideas from all over the world.

Ayumi Hamasaki is Japan's most popular female recording star. She sings J-pop, a fun and lively style of music. You may have heard J-pop without realizing it. It often plays in the background of computer games and cartoons from Japan.

In the mid-20th century, teacher Shinichi Suzuki (1898–1998) combined parts of Western and Japanese musical instruction. He believed that children as young as two could play the violin, as long as the instrument was small enough. As the children grew, they could move on to larger versions.

Breath music

The Ainu people of northern Japan make sounds with their breath to create what they call "throat games". People in Siberia and Alaska, who live more than 1,600 kilometres (1,000 miles) away, also perform this music. In these throat games, or *rekkukara*, singers take turns making each sound. Imagine that you and a friend are singing every other word of a song you both know. The audience must listen very hard and put the pieces together to understand the song.

Island cultures

South of Japan are several more groups of islands. Often, island cultures remain isolated from other cultures for hundreds of years. Music in such places can be quite unlike music played elsewhere in East Asia. However, islands also attract traders and settlers, who can lend their own sounds to the islands' musical style.

Muslims are the second-largest religious group in the Philippines. This Muslim Filipino woman is making music with an instrument called the *kulingtan*. The *kulingtan* is made up of a row of gongs, and is played like a xylophone.

Music of love

The religion of **Islam** began in the Middle East but eventually travelled thousands of kilometres overseas. One type of Malaysian music is *ghazal*, which means "love poems" in Arabic. The *ghazal* came from the Islamic Middle East and is popular at celebrations such as weddings.

Combining East and West

In the AD 200s, Malay settlers began to arrive in the Philippines from the south. More than 1,000 years later, Spain took over the Philippines and controlled it for 300 years. Over time, Filipino classical music reflected this mix of cultures in an interesting way. **Composers** created European forms of music like **symphonies**. But they decided to use older, local **rhythms** in these forms.

Many people who live in the country of Malaysia have ancestors from China. Today many younger people there are less interested in traditional Chinese musical forms such as the Peking opera (see page 30). This may be because there are now so many types of music to choose from. Have you heard of the pop group The Beatles? In the 1960s, young Malaysians created a kind of **pop music** called *yeh-yeh*, named after lyrics in The Beatles' song "She Loves You".

The islands of Indonesia

Indonesia is as long as the continent of Europe and has 300 spoken languages! People in Indonesia live on 6,000 different islands, many of which have their own forms of music. These forms include Christian church music, festival songs, guitar music, brass bands, and *gamelan* (see page 16).

Between China and India

Laos, Cambodia, and Thailand are on a **peninsula** south of China. Their music and dance have a lot in common. The most popular Laotian folk instrument, the *khaen*, is also widely used in Thailand.

Let's dance!

The sound of Cambodia's *pinpeat* orchestras comes from heavy **percussion**. These orchestras provide the music for traditional dancing. They also play at religious ceremonies and other important events. A *pinpeat* uses gongs and drums to create lively music. The *sralai*, a **wind instrument**, is the only non-percussion instrument used.

Pinpeat orchestras such as this one accompany *khmer*, a form of classical dance from Cambodia.

Hidden singers

In Thailand, traditional musicians always supply the background music in the theatre. *Khon* is a type of Thai drama in which actors wear fancy and colourful masks. Because the actors must not speak, an offstage **chorus** sings all the songs and says all the dialogue! That doesn't mean the actors have an easy job. Since they cannot use facial expressions, they rely on gestures to show their emotions. The musicians help the audience follow what is happening by playing music that matches the actors' feelings. There are 100 different demon masks in *khon*. Mask-makers have to follow strict rules when creating them. Demons must show off their teeth, which can look like straight fangs or curving tusks. Their mouths must be snarling or tightly shut. Also, demons may have either bulging eyes or partly closed crocodile eyes.

Totsakan (top right in this photograph) is the most important demon in *khon*. When he is being nice, he wears a mask with smaller teeth! His crown has three levels, with a total of ten faces.

Musical materials

How and why do people make music in East Asia? Are the answers the same as in the rest of the world? Are the answers even the same in each East Asian country? People in China may make music differently from their neighbours in Japan. Let's take a look at some of the ideas behind the region's unique sounds.

Getting in tune

One of the most important musical ideas is **pitch**. This means a sound's highness or lowness. When you **tune** instruments, you make sure that each note you play is at the right pitch. East Asian **cultures**, however, sometimes tune their instruments differently from elsewhere in the world. This helps give them their unique sound. East Asian instruments can also be played at different pitches. For example, the *koto* is a long Japanese *zither*. Its flexible tuning allows it to play a wide range of music, in both Eastern and Western styles.

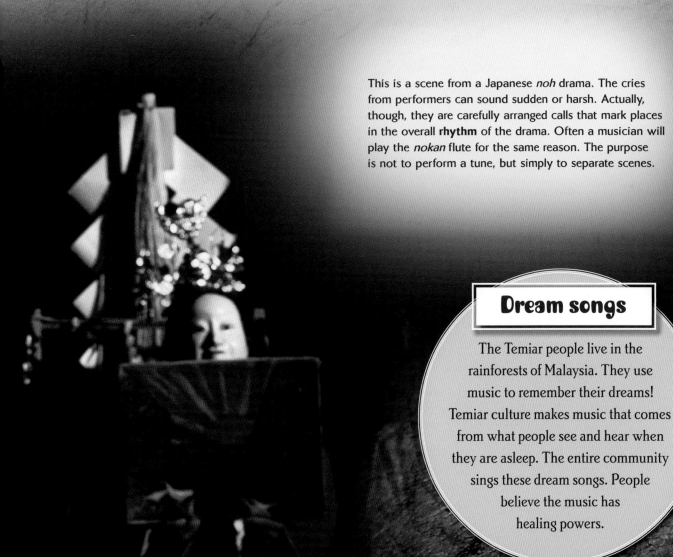

This is a scene from a Japanese *noh* drama. The cries from performers can sound sudden or harsh. Actually, though, they are carefully arranged calls that mark places in the overall **rhythm** of the drama. Often a musician will play the *nokan* flute for the same reason. The purpose is not to perform a tune, but simply to separate scenes.

Dream songs

The Temiar people live in the rainforests of Malaysia. They use music to remember their dreams! Temiar culture makes music that comes from what people see and hear when they are asleep. The entire community sings these dream songs. People believe the music has healing powers.

Keeping the beat

Indonesia's most famous musical groups are the *gamelan*, whose name comes from a word meaning "hammer". *Gamelan* **orchestras** also include metallophones, which are similar to xylophones but with metal bars instead of wood. *Gamelan* instruments can be a lot of fun. Many are so big that you need to sit down to play them. Although these orchestras include stringed instruments and a flute or two, the main sound in a *gamelan* is **percussion**. The drummer is the leader of the group.

At times *gamelan* music can sound repetitive, but that is because it is played in incredibly long loops that can last up to 512 beats. When a new loop begins, it is a slightly different version of the main tune. Indonesians believe that the patience needed by musicians shows their great skill.

Imagine the rhythm of a train chugging along. Then, add pretty chimes to it. That's what a *gamelan* orchestra sounds like!

Special powers

Gamelan orchestras often play at weddings and religious rituals. The *gamelan* instruments themselves are treated with great respect. People believe they have special powers. You must not step over an instrument, as this would be insulting to the spirit that watches over it. In fact, *gamelan* musicians must remove their shoes before playing to make themselves humble. People even offer flowers to the instruments.

Drumbeats across Asia

In many cultures, percussion provides a backbeat for song or dance. In Cambodia, folk dancing in the countryside is often performed to a simple drumbeat with no other instruments. Singers perform Korea's famous *p'ansori* songs (see page 22) accompanied by only a single drummer.

Skull drums

In Tibet, musicians play an hourglass-shaped drum that is made out of human skulls!

Sometimes drummers double as dancers, as in this Korean folk dance. The "farmer's dance" is known for the long ribbons that come from the hat of the leader.

Music for war

During Japan's **Middle Ages**, which began in the 1100s, drumming was an important part of military music. The thundering sound of fast drumming boosted the warriors' fighting spirit before going into battle. Such exciting drumming can be heard today in performances by *taiko* drummers.

There are many similarities between learning *taiko* drumming and martial arts such as judo or karate. The training period for both is long. Balance and precise movements are important in *taiko* drumming and martial arts. You must wear loose clothing and drink plenty of water because each involves a lot of hard work.

When you learn *taiko* drumming, you must also be a good listener. There is no music on paper – all the knowledge is passed along by word of mouth. However, you must also bring earplugs to each lesson to avoid damaging your hearing. This will not block out the noise completely, but it will reduce the sound level.

The ancient Mongols were also spirited warriors who valued music. At one point their empire stretched all the way across Asia. They were excellent riders, and their favourite instrument was a fiddle with a carved horse's head on top called a *morin-khuur*. Although much ancient Mongolian art has been lost, the *morin-khuur* remains a powerful part of the culture even today.

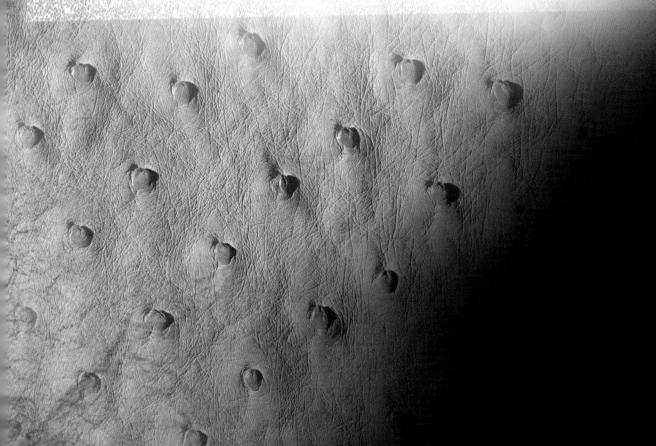

Music for peace

In China, the famous seven-stringed *zither* called the *qin* sounds like a cross between a guitar and a harp. It is usually plucked, but can also be strummed. That means that it can cause the player and the audience to feel many different emotions. You might feel very peaceful and relaxed after listening to a *qin* performance, or you might feel lively and energized.

Chinese people play the *qin* to an audience, for entertainment. But it is also important sometimes to play the *qin* alone. This is because practising the *qin* is believed to make the players better people, helping them to express and control their emotions.

Playing the *qin* is a highly respected skill in China. It demands total control over mind and body.

Bamboo and bone

Like playing the *qin*, mastering the Japanese flute known as the *shakuhachi* is believed to improve the player as a person. The bamboo this flute is made of gives it a wind-like, haunting sound. In Tibet, another **wind instrument** might be "haunting" in a different sense. There, musicians play a kind of trumpet made from a long bone!

Throughout East Asia different materials give instruments their unique sounds. For example, in Malaysia, a percussion instrument called the *raurau* has an interesting sound − it is made from coconut shells.

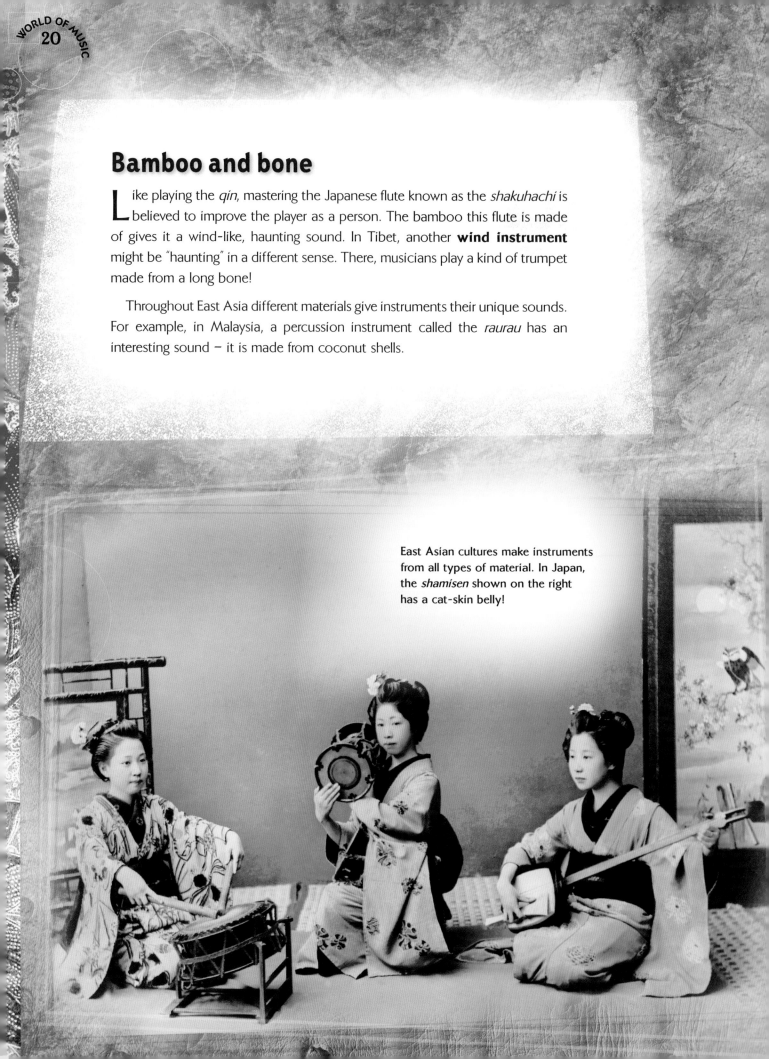

East Asian cultures make instruments from all types of material. In Japan, the *shamisen* shown on the right has a cat-skin belly!

Ivory or plastic?

In ancient China, instruments used to be grouped by their materials. They were divided into silk, skin, and clay instruments. **Ivory** is also a traditional East Asian material, often used for the tuning knobs on stringed instruments. Sometimes ivory was used to make **picks**. Performers wear picks on their fingers like rings. The picks make plucking the strings easier. Other instruments, such as the *shamisen*, have traditionally had a single large pick made of ivory.

Today, modern materials have replaced many of the traditional ones. Workers now use nylon instead of silk for making strings. Similarly, cheap white plastic means there is now less need for ivory. This has many benefits. People are now less likely to hunt elephants for their ivory tusks.

Some instruments are made of wood, but you might not be able to tell! The wooden frame of this harp from Myanmar is covered with gold.

Sharing through song

Important legends are often passed down through songs. In Korea, the *p'ansori* is a type of performance that began 300 years ago. Originally, there were twelve *madang* (the story that each *p'ansori* is based upon), but today only five survive.

P'ansori relies on the talents of a single singer. These performers not only sing, but also tell stories and act them out, taking on the voices of different characters. They hold a folding fan at all times to make their movements larger and more dramatic. By unfolding it, a singer tells the audience that a new scene is about to begin.

The drummer keeps the beat but also makes *chooimsae*. These are verbal sounds of encouragement for the singer. These can be short words or meaningless sounds. The audience members also provide *chooimsae*. This helps the singers keep going when they are tired − one performance can last up to six hours!

The only musical accompaniment for a *p'ansori* singer is a drum.

Stories in music

Folk songs are usually not written down. Instead, they are passed from one performer to another, each one adding new touches. Often folk songs tell a particular story. In China alone there are hundreds of such story-songs in its many towns and villages.

Cruel madang

The *p'ansori madang* "Heungbuga" tells of two brothers: one good and one bad. The younger brother becomes wealthy after helping a bird with a broken leg. His greedy older brother wants to have the same success, so he breaks the leg of a bird on purpose just to fix it!

The Tagalog people of the Philippines perform a range of folk songs, including warrior songs, lullabies, seafaring songs, and love songs.

Singing together

In many countries, people sing their **national anthem** before a sporting event. The Mongols also used to sing special songs before their athletic contests. Singing in **unison** is popular throughout East Asia.

Like folk songs, national anthems help bring people together. In fact, Cambodia's anthem *"Nokoreach"* is based on an older folk song. Often anthems express people's pride in their country. The Philippines were ruled by Spain from 1565 to 1898. During this time, Filipinos had to sing a song in Spanish until a Tagalog version finally became official. Tagalog is the language Filipinos speak.

Here, athletes from Vietnam honour their country by singing their national anthem.

Hold . . . and whistle!

Mongolian *khommei* is a kind of throat singing. Throat singers hold a long, deep note in their chest while making a high whistling sound with their nose and throat. When doing this, they are actually singing two notes at the same time. The song ends up sounding like more than one person is singing it!

Whistle while you work

In China, singing is a big part of everyday life. Singing groups perform at different events in the community. Some groups of people have huge song festivals every year, and many songs are tied to specific jobs such as farming.

In Japan, the Chinese notion of work songs has been taken much further. There, employees sometimes sing company songs to inspire teamwork, loyalty, and *shafu*, a word that means "company spirit". Companies even employ songwriters from other companies to write such songs for them.

Unseen powers

Throughout East Asia, people use music to connect with invisible forces. Japan's oldest religion, Shintoism, has nature gods that are worshipped at **shrines** throughout the country. *Kagura*, or "god music", is performed during Shinto rituals. In addition to playing flutes and hand-held gongs, musicians use *suzu*, a group of tiny bells that are shaken together. Music also plays a key role during Shinto folk festivals. People set up stalls along the street that leads to the shrine. Then, dancers perform to religious chanting.

The magic of a mudang

In Korea, a female religious leader known as a *mudang* uses chanting and music to try to communicate with unseen beings. The *mudang* is also a fortune teller who believes she can communicate with the spirits of people who have died. During one ritual called *kut*, she goes into a **trance** as she dances and sings to contact the spirit world. The *kut* features bright costumes and dancing with flags and swords to the sound of gongs and drums. It is often performed in small family settings.

Sometimes, though, a *mudang* does not go into a trance at all. Instead she lets a spirit take over the body of an audience member. This person then attempts to communicate with the spirit by shaking a basket to answer the *mudang*'s questions.

Travelling gods

Shinto festivals often feature portable shrines. That way, people can take the gods out into the community. There, they visit shops or homes to try to purify them.

Dancing beasts

Chinese communities all over the world celebrate the new year. People parade down city streets to the lively music of drums and gongs. Colourful paper dragons and lions are made to dance to the **rhythm**. As many as 50 people at a time work together to bring these paper beasts to life with exciting movement.

These Chinese dragons are part of the Chingay parade in Singapore. The Chingay parade takes place every year and celebrates Chinese New Year.

Living in harmony

Musical ideas often reflect people's thoughts about how best to live. In Japan, a version of **Buddhism** known as Zen has had a deep impact on music. Zen focuses on simplicity. In some ways *Noh* theatre, with its empty stage and "bare-bones" music, is very simple. But the music and scenery are still important. People believe that these can be more powerful when they are not overdone. A single beat from a hip − or shoulder − drum, or a simple note blown on the *nokan* flute, often carries a lot of meaning.

This bell hangs from the roof of Nanzenji temple in Kyoto, Japan. In Buddhist temples like this one, the sound of bells signifies the end of the last year and the start of the next.

The music of poetry

Temple bells die out.

The fragrant blossoms remain.

A perfect evening!

-Basho (1644−1694)

Zen poets often used a form known as **haiku**. Here a *haiku* by the poet Basho captures the simple sound of temple bells ringing out.

Here, Tibetan monks engage in deep voice chanting in a temple in Lhasa, Tibet.

Prize shakuhachi

Zen had a major impact on the thoughts and feelings of Japan's famous *samurai* warriors. The very simple *shakuhachi* became their special instrument. Apart from monks, nobody was allowed to use this bamboo flute. Playing it was a skill that *samurai* came to prize much like their fighting skills.

Deep voice, one voice

People in Mongolia and parts of western China have followed a form of Buddhism even longer than the Japanese have practised Zen. Known as Tibetan Buddhism, this religion has inspired many great works of art. Its group chants have a deep tone that seems to come from the centre of the Earth. More amazing still, this low-**pitched**, **vibrating** sound sometimes sounds as if it is made by a single voice.

Music in the theatre

In East Asia different types of theatre often have music alongside the performances. In many **cultures**, clowns and dancing storytellers perform with music playing to match the action. In Myanmar, more complex music helps set the tone for each scene.

Peking opera

China's most famous type of theatre is *jingxi*, also called Peking opera or Beijing opera. (China's capital, Beijing, was once known as Peking.) The word "opera" may make you think of Western forms, which can be slow. Peking opera, on the other hand, is high-energy, exciting entertainment that frequently includes martial arts. *The Monkey King* is one story in Peking opera. It is about a legendary superhero who battles against fire, rocks, wind, and enemies, and can leap thousands of kilometres!

During a performance, the **orchestra** sits to the side of the stage and provides exciting music that carries the story along. Gongs, clappers, and cymbals are joined by Chinese fiddles and banjos. The amazing sound they create can be very surprising − a relaxing tune might be followed by a sudden "bang"! The instruments also make sound effects such as the sounds of horses or roosters.

Jackie Chan

Film star Jackie Chan (born 1954) spent 10 years of his childhood training in the Peking opera. There, he learned acrobatic skills that he used in films such as *Rush Hour* and *Shanghai Noon*. Chan is well known for doing his own death-defying stunts.

Kabuki theatre

For a long time, there were no women in Peking opera, so some of its biggest stars were men singing in high-**pitched** voices! In Japan's *kabuki* theatre, female performers faced a similar situation. Although many of its earliest actors were women, in 1629 it became illegal for them to perform. But in 1652, the boys who had taken their parts were also kept from the stage. Older men finally took over the roles. Despite the ban on female performers being lifted around 200 years later, the tradition of an all-male cast in the *kabuki* theatre has remained to this day.

The National Beijing Opera Company of China practises *The Legend of White Snake*. The performers all wear something on their heads. If they didn't, that would be a sign to the audience that a character was in danger.

East Asian puppetry

Throughout East Asia, puppet dramas entertain audiences of all ages. Music is a central part of these shows.

Bunraku, Japan's puppet theatre, features the same instrument as the non-puppet *kabuki* theatre, the *shamisen*. *Bunraku* presents tales full of deep feeling that are often quite sad. In traditional Korean puppetry (*kkoktu kaksi*), the stories are more comical. However, in both styles, music accompanies the lines delivered by the puppet master, who moves the puppets' arms from below with strings.

Puppetry is also extremely popular in Southeast Asia. On the Indonesian island of Java, the puppet master conducts the *gamelan* orchestra so that it knows when to play. However, in addition to being a bandleader, he must control all the puppets and speak the dialogue. If you think that sounds difficult, also remember that these performances can last a whole night!

This is a *bunraku* performance in Kumamoto, Japan. The puppet masters are on stage, dressed in black, so that they can control the almost life-size puppets.

Water puppets

In Vietnam's *muá rôi nuoc* puppet theatre, the stage is the surface of a pond. How do the puppet masters remain dry? They stay far from the action, moving the puppets by using long underwater tubes. These tubes are made of hollow bamboo, which protects the strings inside them that are attached to the puppets.

In Indonesian shadow puppetry, the audience watches images of the puppets cast on to a screen. The puppets are made from the hides of water buffalo. A buffalo horn is used as their main support.

Today's sounds

Modern communication, travel, and technology have all helped create new types of music. Today, East Asian **cultures** interact more with each other — and with the rest of the world — than in past centuries.

Borrowing from the West

In China in the 1800s, Western musical forms such as opera became very popular, and so did non-Asian instruments. Traditional Chinese **composers** and musicians also took up Western musical ideas, such as blending the sounds of instruments in an **orchestra**. Some Chinese people wanted to protect their native music from these outside ideas. They claimed that mixing styles from different places created music that wasn't **authentic**. However, **Western music** has also been influenced by East Asia. Indonesia's *gamelan* music inspired many modern Western composers. Its instruments are often used in music lessons in the West.

An Indonesian ruler in the 1900s outlawed Western music such as rock and roll. As a result, an exciting type of music called *jaipongan* sprang up that didn't use instruments from the West, or even from nearby Japan and China. As it uses tricky **rhythms**, *jaipongan* may not sound like other dance music you've heard. However, it was very popular for dancing in the 1970s. *Jaipongan* features songs with modern lyrics that are backed by a traditional *gamelan* orchestra.

China's *tam-tam* is a large gong that became a part of Western orchestras in the 1800s.

Recordings allow musical styles to spread more quickly. This Laotian store shows the many choices listeners can enjoy.

New music in Vietnam

In the 1920s a new type of opera appeared in Vietnam called *Cai Luong*. Its stories are based on European comedies, but its songs, called *vong co*, are Vietnamese. When an audience hears the start of a popular *vong co* song, it's not unusual for people to start clapping immediately.

New audiences, new choices

As East Asia entered modern times, audiences changed along with the music. Like elsewhere in the world, the huge popularity of the cinema meant traditional theatre and live music became less popular. While the Peking opera still plays to packed houses, for less money audiences can see a similar blend of martial arts and comedy in Hong Kong films. Hong Kong films became popular all over the world in the late 1900s.

However, hit films and television shows in places such as Korea and Japan include dramas set in long-ago time periods. These stories sometimes need traditional music, which means there is still a demand for classically trained composers and musicians.

What connection do modern films have with concerts such as this one? This Chinese singer is performing a song from the film *Crouching Tiger, Hidden Dragon*.

New attitudes

In some places, it's not so much the music that has changed, but people's attitudes towards it. For instance, in Indonesia it has only been during the last century that musicians have started bowing and audiences have started applauding!

East Asia goes global

Easier, faster travel and the spread of musical education have led to more choices for performers. East Asian orchestras now often tour neighbouring countries as well as ones on the other side of the world. This kind of travel helps bring music to new audiences all the time. In addition, gifted musicians no longer play music from only their own cultures. Some of today's best Western **classical music** performers come from East Asia.

This is Seiji Ozawa, conducting at the Boston Symphony Hall in 2000. He is one of many East Asian musicians who have had international success.

Seiji Ozawa

Seiji Ozawa (born 1935) had dreams of becoming a concert pianist until a sporting injury left him with broken fingers on both hands. That's when he decided to try **conducting**. After winning awards in France and studying briefly in Germany, Ozawa became the Boston Symphony Orchestra's music director.

Singing with machines

Technology has also changed the roles of the performer and the audience. *Karaoke* is a Japanese word meaning "empty orchestra". A *karaoke* singer seems to be performing with an actual musical group. However, *karaoke* machines are more like jukeboxes with microphones. Singers read lyrics on a video screen and do their best to keep time with the pre-recorded music. While *karaoke* machines can be found all over the world, in Japan they are sometimes in surprising places, such as taxis!

In some ways, *karaoke* is just as important to work as it is to play. In Japan, workers feel a strong connection to their companies. Teamwork is often put ahead of personal goals. In order to build this sense of everyone working together, people from the same office frequently spend time together long after the working day is over. *Karaoke* plays a major part in these outings, allowing businesspeople to unwind and have fun together.

These men are enjoying *karaoke* in Tokyo, Japan. *Karaoke* can let terrible singers be heard in public, but it also provides entertainment for the listeners!

Electronic beats

Although it began in the West, techno music has become popular in East Asia. This kind of rhythm-centred dance music uses computer and sound equipment, much of which is produced in the region. Japan, in particular, is responsible for creating many new types of **synthesizer** music. Techno music changes with every new electronic product that is developed.

Shown in the white cap, DJ Cake is very popular in Cambodia. Here, he encourages a dance crowd. Though technology keeps changing, the idea of bringing people together through dance never goes away.

Lee Jung Hyun

Techno artist Lee Jung Hyun (born 1980) is a Korean singer who is popular across Asia. Although her music uses strange sounds like sirens, the catchy tunes are good for dancing. Hyun has recorded many of her hits in Japanese as well.

Old or new?

Some cultures accept both the old and the new. For example, in Japan, the rise of radio in the 1920s actually led to the public learning more about old folk songs. In addition, traditional *taiko* drum corps now provide music for films and have their work recorded on CDs. In Korea, the broadcast of *p'ansori* performances into people's homes by radio has not hurt this traditional form of music. Instead, it has helped *p'ansori* reach new audiences.

But these same technologies also help spread brand new forms of music. Some musicians focus on the future, not the past. The Japanese pop band Polysics, for instance, goes out of its way to show off its science-fiction look. They create music with computers, synthesizers, and **vocoder technology** that changes the human voice. Polysics is an example of how East Asian music is popular with a worldwide audience. The band releases its recordings not only in Japan, but also in Korea and the United States.

This troupe of dancers and musicians performs
in traditional costumes across Thailand.

Open orchestra

In 2003, the traditional Hong Kong Chinese Orchestra opened a music festival by inviting 3,000 citizens to participate in drumming for a piece titled *The Earth Shall Move*. Events such as this show that traditional instruments and music remain strong in East Asia.

Compare the unusual outfits of Polysics and those shown on the opposite page. Is one of these more East Asian than the other?

New traditions

Think about East Asia's rich musical history. Today's newest music may one day be considered traditional. Gradually, people come to think of new music itself as old-fashioned. Such attitude changes have already taken place over China's long history.

New East Asian music

One of the great things about East Asian music is that there are so many settings in which you can enjoy it. You can watch a colourfully costumed dance troupe perform, or fall under the spell of *taiko* drummers and the shadowy movements of puppet-warriors. You can sit quietly near a temple and listen for the peaceful sound of chanting or bells, or walk down a street in a major city and hear the latest electronic sounds coming out of a music shop or a nightclub. East Asian music means many different things to many people. It is old and new, ancient and modern.

Take a look at the two photos on these pages. Which best represents the heart of East Asian music?

They both do!

These bone flutes, discovered in Jiahu, China, are 9,000 years old. The flute that is second from the bottom is the world's oldest playable instrument!

Hong Kong superstar Andy Lau greets the audience at a concert. Besides being a popular recording artist, Lau is also one of the top film stars in the world.

A world of music

	String Instruments	Brass Instruments	Wind Instruments
Africa	*oud* (lute), *rebec* (fiddle), *kora* (harp-lute), *ngoni* (harp), musical bow, one-string fiddle	*kakakai* or *wazi* (metal trumpets), horns made from animals horns	*naga, nay sodina* (flutes), *arghul, gaita* (single-reed instruments), *mizmar* (double-reed instrument)
Australia, Hawaii, and the Pacific	ukulele (modern), guitar (modern)		flutes, nose flutes, didgeridoo, conch shell horns
Eastern Asia	*erhu* (fiddle), *dan tranh, qin, koto, gayageum* (derived from **zithers**)	gongs, metallophones, xylophones	*shakuhachi* (flute), *khaen* (mouth organ), *sralai* (reed instrument)
Europe	violin, viola, cello, double bass, mandolin, guitar, lute, *zither*, hurdy gurdy (folk instruments)	trumpet, French horn, trombone, tuba	flute, recorder, oboe, clarinet, bassoon, bass clarinet, saxophone, accordion, bagpipes
Latin America and the Caribbean	*berimbau* (musical bow), *guitarrón* (bass guitar), *charango* (mandolin), *vilhuela* (high-**pitched** guitar)	trumpet, saxophone, trombone (salsa)	*bandoneon* (button accordion)
Western Asia	*sitar, veena, oud, dombra, doutar, tar* (lutes), *rebab, kobyz* (fiddles), *sarod, santoor, sarangi*	trumpets	*bansuri, ney* (flutes), *pungi/been* (clarinets), *shehnai, sorna* (oboes)

Percussion Instruments	Vocal Styles	Dance Styles
balafon (wooden xylophone), *mbira* (thumb piano), bells, slit drums, friction drums, hourglass drums, conventional drums	open throat singing, Arabic style singing: this is more nasal (in the nose), and includes many trills and ornaments	spiritual dancing, mass dances, team/formation dances, small group and solo dances, modern social dances
drums, slit drums, rattles, clapsticks, gourds, rolled mats	*oli* (sung by one person), *mele* (poetry), hula (type of *mele*), *himene* (choral music), Dreaming songs	hula (accompanies song), seated dances, *fa'ataupati* (clapping and slapping), haka (chant)
taiko (drums)	*p'ansori* (single singer), *chooimsae* (verbal encouragement), folk songs	Peking/Beijing opera, Korean folk dance
side drum, snare drum, tambourine, *timpani* (kettle drums), cymbals, castanets, bodhran, piano	solo ballad, work song, hymn, *plainchant* (religious singing), opera, Music Hall, cabaret, choral, homophony (harmony, parts moving together), polyphony (independent vocals together)	jig, reel, sword dance, clog dance, *mazurka* (folk dances), flamenco, country dance, waltz, polka, ballet, *pavane, galliard* (16th century)
friction drum, steel drums, bongos (small drums), congas (large drums), *timbales* (shallow drums), maracas (shakers), *guiro* (scraper)	toasting	*zouk* (pop music), tango, lambada, samba, *bossa nova* (city music), rumba, mambo, *merengue* (salsa)
tabla drum, *dhol* drum, tambourine, *bartal* cymbals, bells, sticks, gongs	bards, *qawwali* (Sufi music), throat singing, *ghazals* (love poem)	*bhangra* (Punjabi dance), *dabke* (traditional), Indian classical, whirling dervishes, belly dancing

Glossary

authentic something that sticks to its traditional origins. This could be music, or a different form of expression.

Buddhism major world religion that began in India around 500 BC

chorus group of singers or actors who perform together

classical music music which is composed and written down, usually played by trained musicians

composer person who writes music

conduct lead the performance of a piece of music, usually in an orchestra or choir

culture music, art, customs, and religion of a people

ethnic group people who share the same language or background within a larger group or country

folk music music played by everyday people, often in informal settings

haiku Japanese poem of seventeen syllables, in three lines of five, seven, and then five again

Islam major world religion that began in Arabia around AD 600

ivory hard, white material found in the tusks of animals such as elephants

Middle Ages period of history. Japan's Middle Ages started around 1185 and ended in the 1800s.

Muslim person who follows Islam

national anthem official song of a country, usually sung at special events

orchestra large group of instruments played by trained musicians

peninsula land mass that extends out into a body of water

percussion musical instrument that makes sound when it is shaken or struck

pick small, hard device that musicians use to pluck strings

pitch highness or lowness of a sound

pop music short for "popular music", it is often played by young people

rhythm how musical notes are placed over time

shrine holy place

symphony long musical piece for an orchestra to perform

synthesizer machine that makes or changes sounds

trance being unaware of your surroundings. When people are in a trance, it looks like they are in a deep sleep.

tune adjust the source of sound to produce a certain pitch

unison several people doing something all together, such as singing

vibrate move back and forth rapidly. In music, vibrations occur when an item such as a string is released.

vocoder technology technology that allows instruments to take on the traits of human speech, and has often been used to make singing sound "robotic"

Western music music that comes from Europe and North and South America

wind instrument instrument that produces sound when air is blown into it

zither plucked stringed instrument without a long neck

Further information

Books

Destination Detectives: China, Ali Brownlie Bojang
(Raintree, 2007)

Star Files: Jackie Chan, Dan Fox (Raintree, 2005)

World Art and Culture: Japanese, Kamini Khanduri
(Raintree, 2003)

Websites

Bayanihan: The Philippine National Folk
Dance Company
www.bayanihannationaldanceco.ph/index.html
Information about Filipino folk dance traditions

The Hong Kong Chinese Orchestra
www.hkco.org/eng/about_hkco_eng.asp
This traditional group has performed throughout
East Asia and in the United Kingdom, Australia,
Canada, and the United States.

Jackie Chan
www.jackiechankids.com
Information about Jackie Chan's childhood days
at the China Drama Academy, where he was
trained in Peking opera

The Music Department of Wesleyan University
http://learningobjects.wesleyan.edu/vim/
This has audio and video samples, as well
as detailed descriptions and histories of
the instruments.

Recordings

*Kim So-hee: P'ansori—Korea's Epic Vocal Art
& Instrumental Music,* Various (Wea, 1990)

Music of Indonesia series, Various (Smithsonian
Folkways, 1990–1999)

Sacred Tibetan Chant , The Monks of Sherab Ling
Monastery (Naxos World, 2003)

Museums

The British Museum
Great Russell Street
London, WCIB 3DG
The museum has a permanent collection
of artefacts from China, Japan, Korea, and
Central and South-east Asia.
www.thebritishmuseum.ac.uk

Live performances

The Hong Kong Chinese Orchestra
www.hkco.org/eng/about_hkco_eng.asp
The Hong Kong Chinese Orchestra gives
performances all around the world. Email
inquiries@hkco.org to find out details of their
latest concerts.

Index